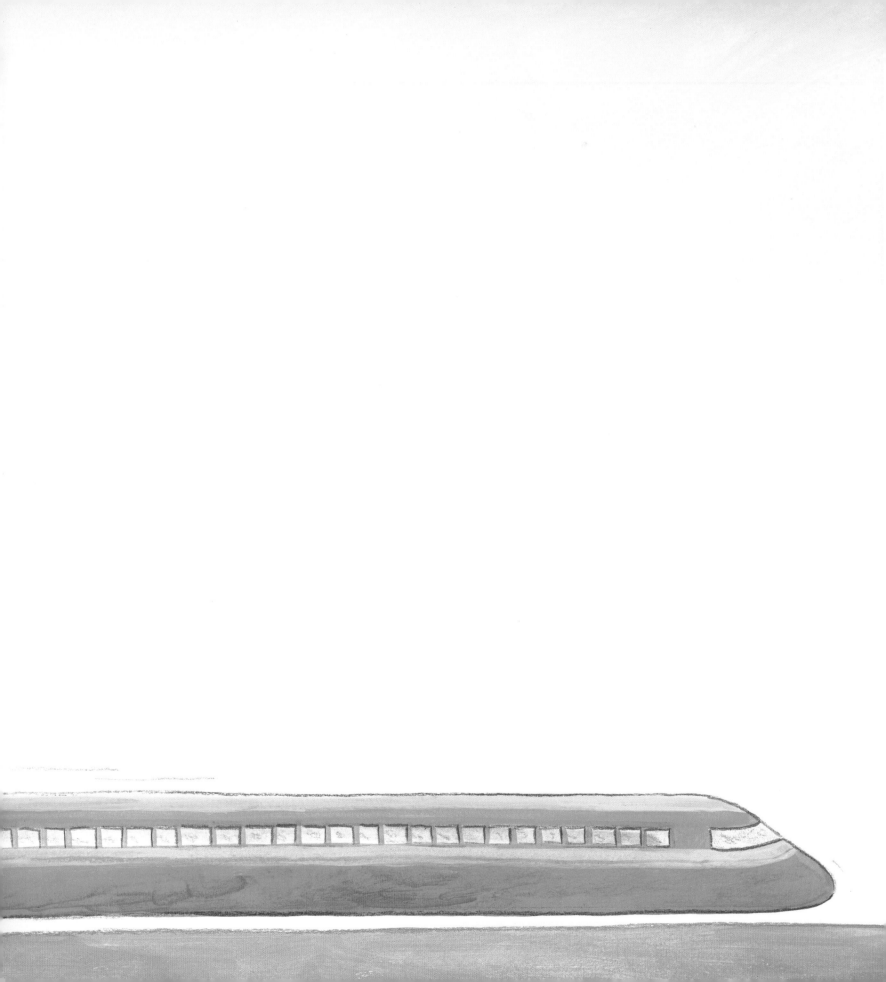

Want to know
the world

Traveling by Train

Pierre Winters & Tineke Meirink

Clavis

NEW YORK

Choo-choo…. TOOT TOOT! Sam is playing with his train. He lines up all his cars. The first car is the locomotive. When that one starts, the other ones follow. Gee, Sam would really like to be in one of these trains himself! But he's too big, of course....

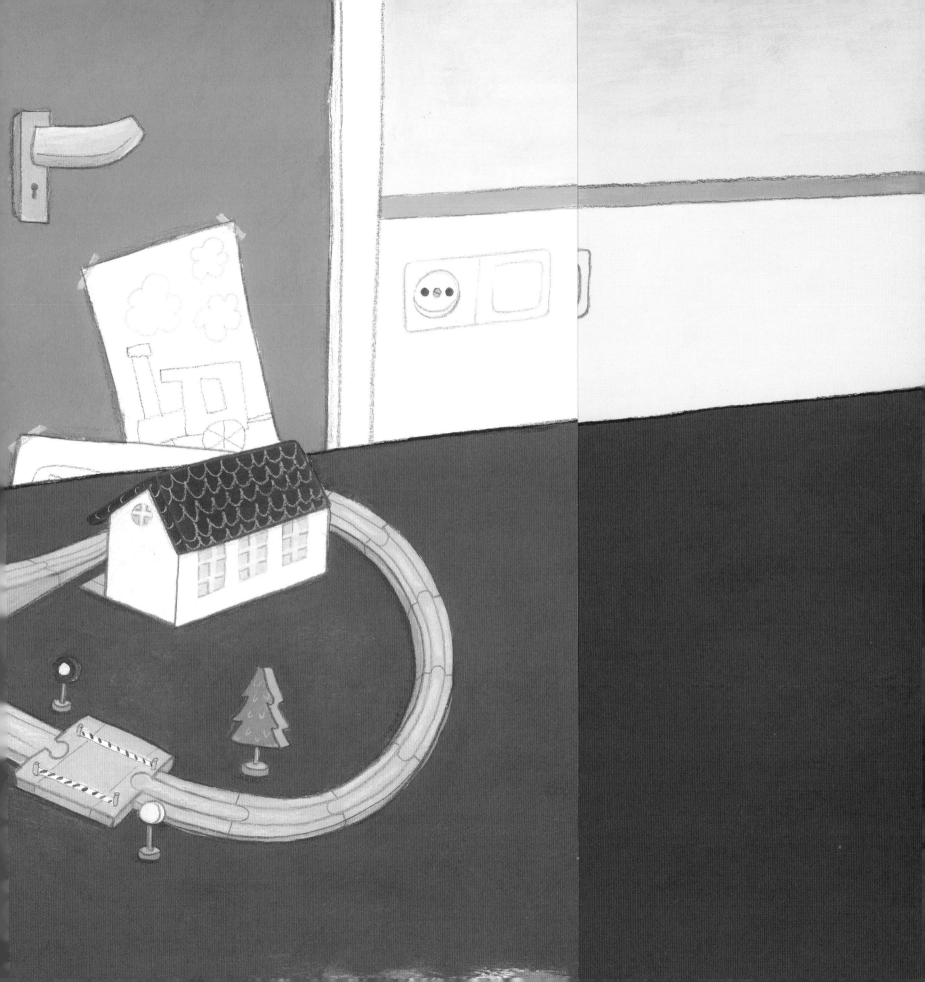

Modern trains and old trains

The very first trains ran on steam. Coal was burned in a big furnace in order to heat a kettle filled with water. The water evaporated and became steam. The steam set the wheels in motion. And that's how the train moved. Wow, that's complicated!

Old steam train

Steam trains were actually meant to transport things, but sometimes naughty people jumped on board too! Only later were trains made especially for people. They had little balconies to stand on and the cars were closed off. That was safer. But there were windows too, so passengers could still enjoy the view.

Did you know many people were afraid of the first trains? They made so much noise and went so fast.... Even though trains back then could only go thirty miles per hour!

Steam train for people

Old-fashioned diesel train

Steam trains produce a lot of dirty, stinky smoke. That's why trains later started running on diesel, which is a little cleaner. More and more trains were built, so more and more tracks were needed.

Electric train

Most of the trains you see today are electric trains. They run on electricity through the wires that hang above the tracks. Every day, they bring thousands of people to work or take them on holidays. These trains are quieter, less polluting and faster.

High-speed train

The newest trains are really fast. They sometimes drive nearly two hundred miles per hour. That's three times faster than a car on the highway. That's why they're called high-speed trains.

Trains are everywhere

There are trains all over the world. They come in all kinds of shapes and sizes.

Tunnel train

You can even go underwater by train! There is
a long tunnel under the sea between England and France.
You can go through it in a car, but only if you park that car
in a very special train. So actually, you're going
by car and by train at the same time.

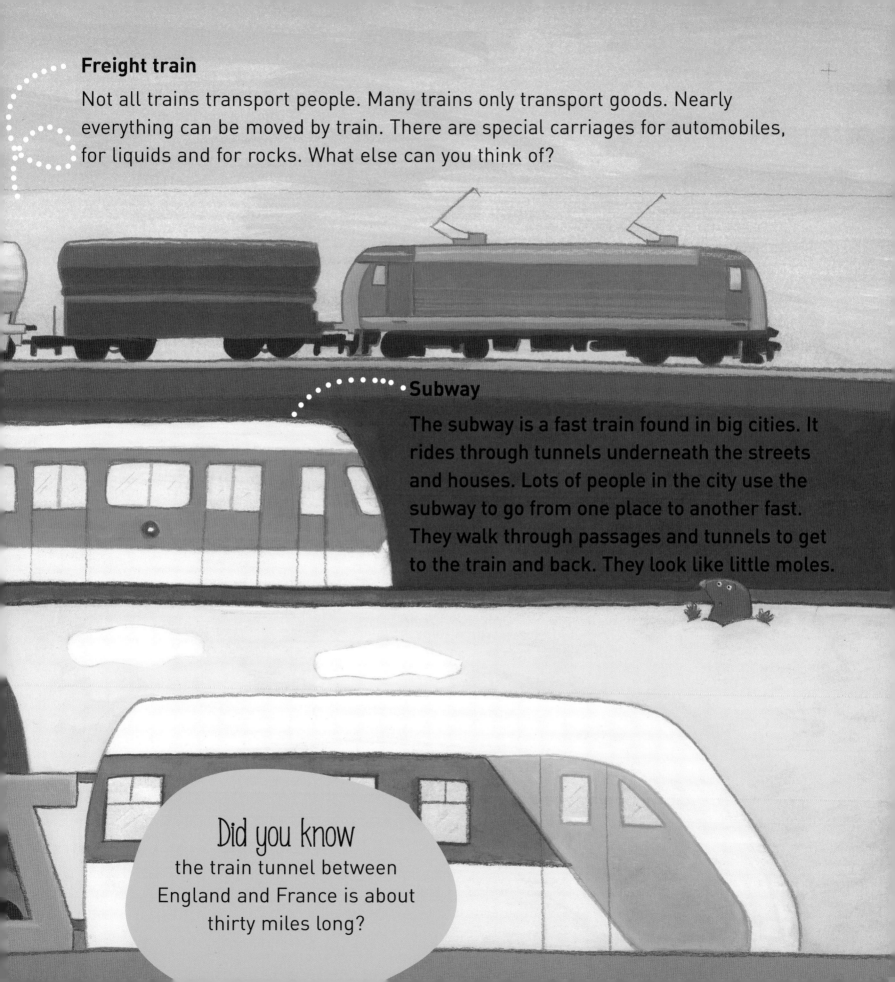

Freight train

Not all trains transport people. Many trains only transport goods. Nearly everything can be moved by train. There are special carriages for automobiles, for liquids and for rocks. What else can you think of?

Subway

The subway is a fast train found in big cities. It rides through tunnels underneath the streets and houses. Lots of people in the city use the subway to go from one place to another fast. They walk through passages and tunnels to get to the train and back. They look like little moles.

Did you know the train tunnel between England and France is about thirty miles long?

Many people work for the railroad

Maintenance workers make sure the trains and tracks are in good shape. They clean and fix things.

The engineer is a kind of driver. He drives the train and stops for the red lights.

The conductor makes sure everyone gets on and off the train all right. She also checks if you have a valid ticket.

Trains often have to drive from one track to the other using something called a switch. **The signalman** sets the switches and makes all the traffic lights turn green or red. This is an important job, because little mistakes can cause big collisions if trains drive on the wrong track!

A modern passenger train - the inside

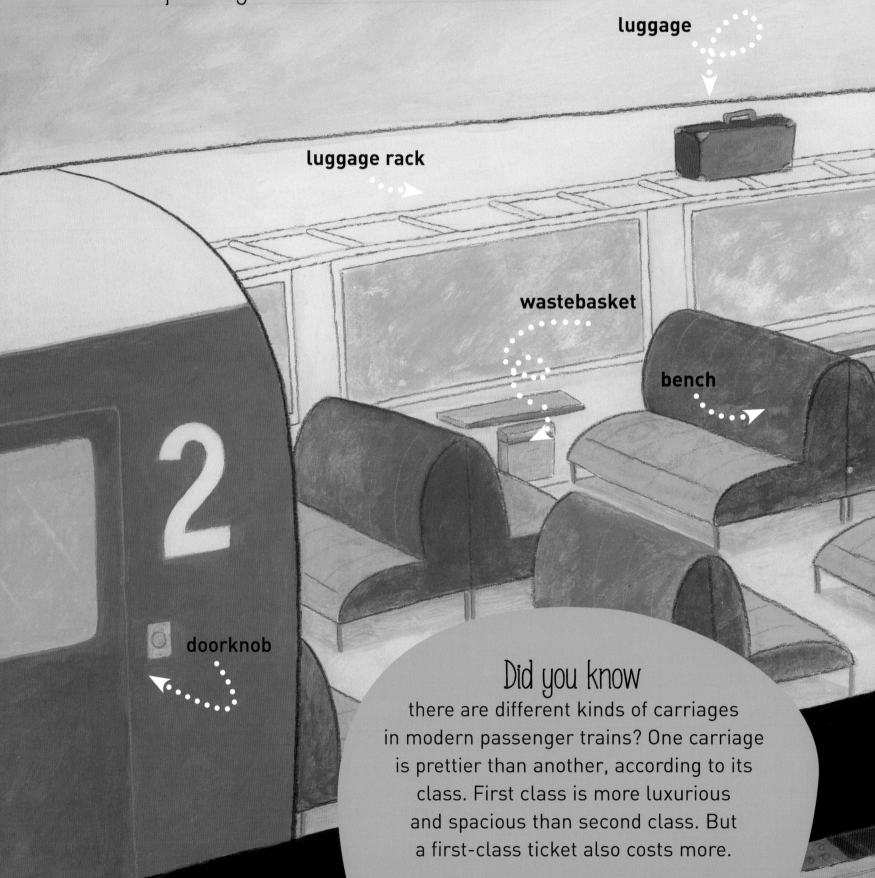

luggage

luggage rack

wastebasket

bench

2

doorknob

Did you know
there are different kinds of carriages in modern passenger trains? One carriage is prettier than another, according to its class. First class is more luxurious and spacious than second class. But a first-class ticket also costs more.

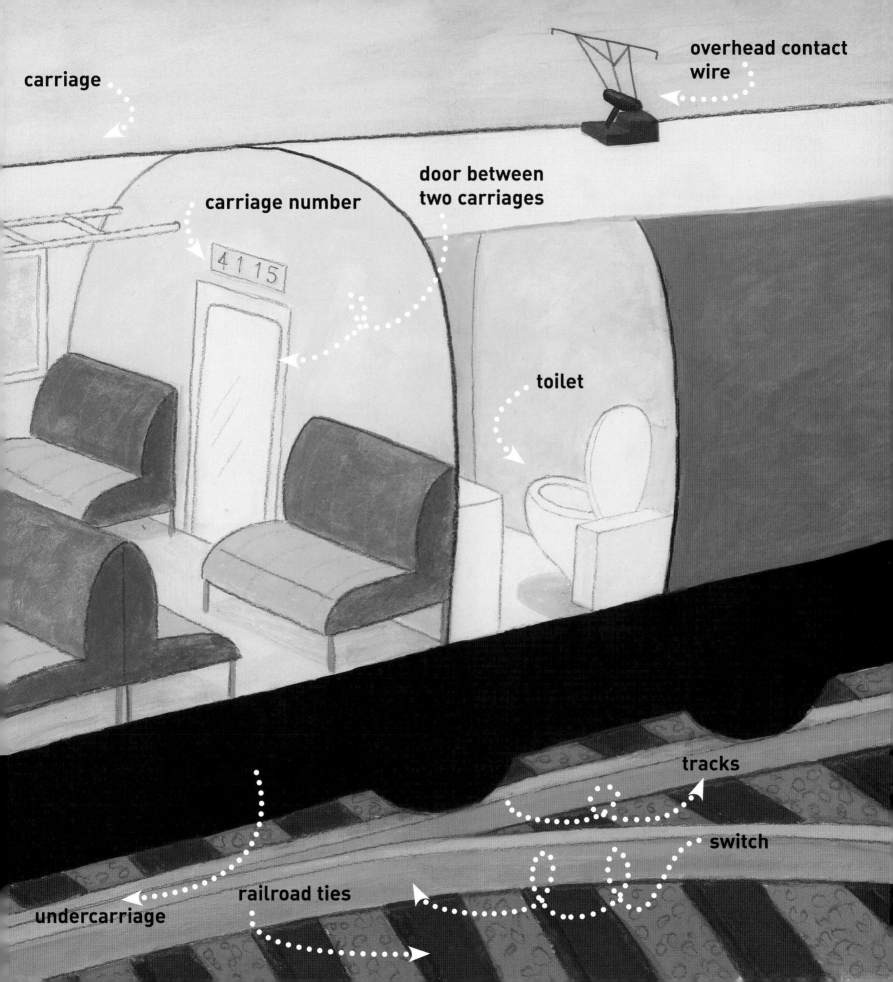

Missing the train

YOU HAVE TO LEAVE IN TIME WHEN YOU WANT TO TRAVEL BY TRAIN, BECAUSE THE TRAIN WON'T WAIT FOR YOU. SO MAKE SURE YOU HAVE EVERYTHING YOU NEED, OTHERWISE...

OOPS... MISSED THE TRAIN!

newsstand

sandwich bar

platform

tracks

In most stations, you can also get something to eat or drink. Some people have to travel by train for hours. They're really hungry when they arrive! But conductors and engineers sometimes want to drink a nice cup of coffee too.

Did you know
you can recognize a conductor by his hat? Most of the time, the conductor also carries a whistle. When you hear that sound, the train is leaving!

At the station

Sometimes the train is late. This is called a delay. People have to wait longer for their train then. Fortunately, they can go to the shop to buy a newspaper or a magazine. That way, they can read and pass the time.

ticket machine

information board with departures

Exactly on time

Trains don't run at any old time. They leave the station exactly at the scheduled time, and they arrive at another station at an exact time too. These departure and arrival times are fixed, so you have to make sure that you're at the right platform at the right time…. Otherwise the train will just leave without you. Trains don't always go to the city where you want to go. Sometimes you have to change from one train to another at a station. You have to check in advance if you have enough time to get from one train to the other. This is called a connection.

Buying a ticket

Of course, you have to pay to travel by train. You do that by buying a ticket. You can buy one over the internet, at the ticket machine or at the ticket office. The conductor will come by on the train to check if you have a valid ticket.

Did you know

someone who rides the train without a ticket is called a "fare dodger"? Riding without a ticket is illegal, so that person will be fined.

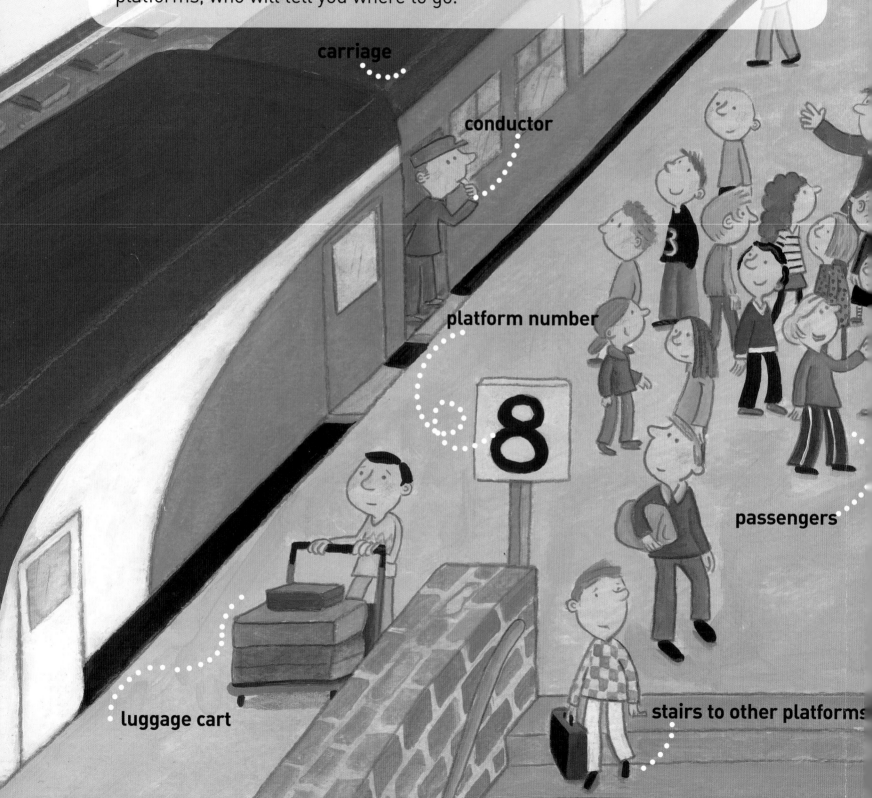

Pay attention! There are often many tracks and trains in one station. You have to be careful, or you might get on the wrong train. Luckily there are big signs that show you which trains you have to take. Often there are conductors on the platforms, who will tell you where to go.

carriage

conductor

platform number

8

passengers

luggage cart

stairs to other platforms

locomotive

All kinds of trains

There are different kinds of trains in every corner of the world. Some trains travel such long distances that they need more than one day to reach their destination. We call that an overnight train and you can often sleep in such a train. When night falls, you can turn the benches into beds and have a sleepover on the tracks!

Did you know
there are even trains with bedrooms, restaurants and little shops? They are like hotels on wheels!

In countries such as India and in some areas of Africa the train is often the only way to get from the countryside to the city. The travelers are desperate to get on board, even when the train is already jam-packed. They hold on to the exterior or climb up on the roof. Sometimes they also bring their animals along. Very dangerous!

In Japan there are very modern trains, such as trains without a driver. A computer knows exactly when everyone has gotten on and where the station is. Other trains don't even use wheels anymore. Thanks to very powerful magnets, they float just above the ground!

A modern station

Modern stations are often very pretty. Most are big buildings, and some are made almost entirely out of glass. You can get your ticket from a machine, and a big electronic board shows you when your train is leaving. Sometimes the trains go underground. Then you can take the stairs or an elevator to get to your platform. It is often very busy at modern stations, with many people and many trains. All kinds of things are happening and there is a lot to see.

Did you know

the biggest train station in the world is in America? In New York City, there is a station with 44 platforms and 67 tracks. Good luck finding your way around there!

Traveling by train

Such a hurry, such a hurry.
Look out as I rush by!

To the platform, to the platform.
Onwards and forwards I fly.

Let me through, let me through.
I know where I have to be.

Out of the way, out of the way.
Or the train will leave without me!

We are a train

With choo-choo-chairs,
you can make a real train.
Everyone get in!

In front sits the engineer.
He drives the train
very precisely.

And there is the conductor.
He punches our tickets.
The rest of us are passengers.

Do you want to draw a train yourself? You can do it step by step.

1 Draw a long rectangle with a square next to it.

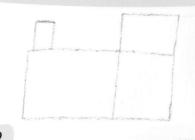

2 Put a little tower on the rectangle and a box on the square.

3 Make wheels! And put a small rectangle to the right of the square. Do you see the train yet?

4 Draw a smoke stack and half a circle on the left. Make a window and a small roof on the right.

5 Finish the front of the train and draw a line above the wheels.

6 Choo-choo... toot-toot!

Make your own conductor's whistle!

With a pair of scissors, some glue, a pencil and a piece of paper, you too can be a conductor. You can decide when the train leaves with your very own conductor's whistle! (Ask your mom or dad for some help.)

1 Draw a line from the top to the bottom of your paper. Make a half circle in the middle.

2 Cut exactly on the line you drew.

3 Now roll it up!

4 Make sure the little half circle sticks out. This will make the whistling sound.

5 Glue down the edge of the paper.

6 Wait...

7 Get in, everyone! The train is leaving!